50 Camping Cuisine: Easy Outdoor Recipes

By: Kelly Johnson

Table of Contents

- Campfire Breakfast Burritos
- Grilled Foil Pack Potatoes
- Simple S'mores
- One-Pot Chili
- Campfire Quesadillas
- Grilled Veggie Skewers
- Sausage and Peppers Foil Pack
- Easy Campfire Nachos
- Campfire French Toast
- Bacon-Wrapped Hot Dogs
- Grilled Chicken Kebabs
- Campfire Pancakes
- Foil Pack Chicken Fajitas
- Smoky Campfire Baked Beans
- Campfire Pizza
- Grilled Shrimp Tacos
- Campfire Corn on the Cob
- Sausage and Potato Hash
- Campfire Grilled Cheese
- Dutch Oven Mac and Cheese
- Campfire Apple Crisp
- Campfire Burgers
- Grilled Veggie Tacos
- Foil Pack Salmon
- Quick Camping Stir-Fry
- Campfire Popcorn
- Grilled Sausage and Veggie Skewers
- Campfire Breakfast Skillet
- Baked Sweet Potatoes on the Grill
- Campfire Casserole
- Grilled Pineapple with Honey
- Campfire Sandwiches
- Foil Pack Beef Stew
- Skillet Pineapple Chicken
- Camping Caesar Salad

- Grilled Garlic Bread
- Campfire Apple Pie
- Easy Grilled Pork Chops
- Campfire Ribs
- Dutch Oven Beef Stew
- Grilled Peppers and Onions
- Campfire Frittata
- Grilled Avocados with Salsa
- Campfire Beef Tacos
- Quick and Easy Trail Mix
- Campfire Fried Rice
- Grilled Bananas with Chocolate
- Foil Pack Veggie Stir-Fry
- S'mores Nachos
- Campfire Spaghetti

Campfire Breakfast Burritos

Ingredients

- 4 flour tortillas
- 4 eggs, scrambled
- 1 cup shredded cheese
- 1/2 cup cooked bacon or sausage, crumbled
- 1/2 cup salsa
- 1/4 cup sour cream
- Salt and pepper to taste

Instructions

1. Scramble the eggs over the campfire or on a portable stove, adding salt and pepper to taste.
2. Warm the flour tortillas on a grill or over the campfire for a few seconds on each side.
3. Assemble the burritos: add scrambled eggs, cheese, bacon or sausage, salsa, and sour cream to the center of each tortilla.
4. Roll up the tortillas and enjoy hot!

Grilled Foil Pack Potatoes

Ingredients

- 4 medium potatoes, sliced
- 1 tbsp olive oil
- 2 cloves garlic, minced
- 1/2 tsp paprika
- Salt and pepper to taste
- Fresh herbs (optional, like rosemary or thyme)

Instructions

1. Preheat the grill or campfire.
2. Cut the potatoes into thin slices and place them on a large piece of foil.
3. Drizzle with olive oil and sprinkle with garlic, paprika, salt, pepper, and fresh herbs.
4. Fold the foil into a packet, sealing the edges.
5. Grill over medium heat for about 25-30 minutes, flipping halfway through, until the potatoes are tender.
6. Open the foil and serve.

Simple S'mores

Ingredients

- Graham crackers
- Marshmallows
- Milk chocolate bars

Instructions

1. Roast marshmallows over the campfire until golden and melty.
2. Place the roasted marshmallow between two graham cracker squares, adding a piece of chocolate in between.
3. Press together and enjoy this classic campfire treat.

One-Pot Chili

Ingredients

- 1 lb ground beef or turkey
- 1 onion, chopped
- 1 bell pepper, chopped
- 2 cloves garlic, minced
- 1 can (14.5 oz) diced tomatoes
- 1 can (15 oz) kidney beans, drained and rinsed
- 1 can (15 oz) black beans, drained and rinsed
- 1 tbsp chili powder
- 1 tsp cumin
- Salt and pepper to taste
- 1 cup beef or vegetable broth

Instructions

1. In a large pot over the campfire or stove, cook the ground meat until browned.
2. Add the chopped onion, bell pepper, and garlic, cooking until softened.
3. Stir in the tomatoes, beans, chili powder, cumin, salt, and pepper.
4. Add the broth and bring the chili to a simmer.
5. Let it cook for 20-30 minutes, stirring occasionally.
6. Serve hot with optional toppings like sour cream or shredded cheese.

Campfire Quesadillas

Ingredients

- 4 flour tortillas
- 2 cups shredded cheese
- 1/2 cup cooked chicken, beef, or beans
- 1/4 cup salsa
- Butter for grilling

Instructions

1. Heat a skillet or grill over the campfire.
2. Place one tortilla on the grill and sprinkle with cheese, cooked meat or beans, and salsa.
3. Top with another tortilla and cook for 2-3 minutes on each side, until golden and the cheese is melted.
4. Remove from the grill, cut into wedges, and serve.

Grilled Veggie Skewers

Ingredients

- 1 red bell pepper, cut into chunks
- 1 zucchini, sliced
- 1 red onion, cut into chunks
- 1 cup mushrooms, halved
- 1 tbsp olive oil
- Salt and pepper to taste
- Wooden skewers

Instructions

1. Soak the wooden skewers in water for 30 minutes to prevent burning.
2. Thread the veggies onto the skewers, alternating colors.
3. Drizzle with olive oil and season with salt and pepper.
4. Grill the skewers over the campfire for 8-10 minutes, turning occasionally, until the vegetables are tender and slightly charred.
5. Serve hot.

Sausage and Peppers Foil Pack

Ingredients

- 4 sausages (any variety)
- 1 bell pepper, sliced
- 1 onion, sliced
- 1 tbsp olive oil
- 1 tsp Italian seasoning
- Salt and pepper to taste

Instructions

1. Preheat the grill or campfire.
2. Slice the sausages into chunks and place them in the center of a large piece of foil.
3. Add the sliced bell pepper and onion, drizzle with olive oil, and sprinkle with Italian seasoning, salt, and pepper.
4. Fold the foil into a packet and grill for 15-20 minutes, flipping halfway through, until the sausages are cooked through.
5. Open the foil and serve.

Easy Campfire Nachos

Ingredients

- Tortilla chips
- 1 cup shredded cheese
- 1/2 cup salsa
- 1/4 cup sour cream
- Optional toppings: jalapeños, guacamole, beans

Instructions

1. Spread tortilla chips in a cast-iron skillet or foil pan.
2. Top with cheese and any optional toppings.
3. Place the skillet or pan over the campfire or grill, covering it with foil to melt the cheese.
4. After 5-7 minutes, remove from the fire and top with salsa, sour cream, and other toppings.
5. Serve immediately.

Campfire French Toast

Ingredients

- 4 slices of bread
- 2 eggs
- 1/4 cup milk
- 1 tsp vanilla extract
- 1/2 tsp cinnamon
- Butter for cooking
- Maple syrup

Instructions

1. In a bowl, whisk together the eggs, milk, vanilla, and cinnamon.
2. Dip each slice of bread into the egg mixture, coating both sides.
3. Heat butter in a skillet or over a grill and cook each slice of French toast for 2-3 minutes per side, until golden.
4. Serve with syrup and enjoy!

Bacon-Wrapped Hot Dogs

Ingredients

- **4 hot dogs**
- **4 slices bacon**
- **Skewers or grill basket**

Instructions

1. Wrap each hot dog with a slice of bacon, securing it with toothpicks if needed.
2. Preheat your grill or campfire.
3. Skewer the bacon-wrapped hot dogs or place them in a grill basket.
4. Grill the hot dogs over medium heat for about 10-12 minutes, turning frequently, until the bacon is crispy and the hot dogs are heated through.
5. Serve on buns with your favorite toppings.

Grilled Chicken Kebabs

Ingredients

- 2 chicken breasts, cubed
- 1 red bell pepper, chopped
- 1 onion, chopped
- 1 zucchini, sliced
- 2 tbsp olive oil
- 1 tbsp lemon juice
- 1 tsp paprika
- Salt and pepper to taste
- Wooden skewers (soaked in water)

Instructions

1. Preheat your grill or campfire.
2. In a bowl, mix olive oil, lemon juice, paprika, salt, and pepper.
3. Toss the chicken and vegetables in the marinade, ensuring everything is evenly coated.
4. Thread the chicken and veggies onto skewers, alternating the pieces.
5. Grill the kebabs for 10-15 minutes, turning occasionally, until the chicken is cooked through.
6. Serve with rice or flatbreads.

Campfire Pancakes

Ingredients

- 1 cup pancake mix
- 1/2 cup water or milk
- 1 tbsp butter (for cooking)
- Maple syrup

Instructions

1. Preheat a skillet or griddle over the campfire.
2. In a bowl, mix the pancake mix with water or milk to form a batter.
3. Melt a little butter in the skillet and pour the batter into small circles.
4. Cook for 2-3 minutes on each side, flipping when bubbles form on top.
5. Serve with syrup and toppings of your choice.

Foil Pack Chicken Fajitas

Ingredients

- 2 chicken breasts, sliced
- 1 red bell pepper, sliced
- 1 green bell pepper, sliced
- 1 onion, sliced
- 1 tbsp olive oil
- 1 tsp chili powder
- 1 tsp cumin
- Salt and pepper to taste
- Tortillas (for serving)

Instructions

1. Preheat the grill or campfire.
2. In a bowl, toss the chicken, peppers, onion, olive oil, chili powder, cumin, salt, and pepper.
3. Lay out a large piece of foil and spread the mixture evenly in the center.
4. Fold the foil into a packet, sealing the edges.
5. Grill the foil pack for 20-25 minutes, turning occasionally, until the chicken is cooked through.
6. Serve with tortillas and your favorite fajita toppings.

Smoky Campfire Baked Beans

Ingredients

- 2 cans (15 oz each) baked beans
- 1/2 cup barbecue sauce
- 1 tbsp mustard
- 1/2 cup chopped onions
- 1/4 cup cooked bacon, crumbled

Instructions

1. Preheat the campfire or grill to medium heat.
2. In a pot, mix the baked beans, barbecue sauce, mustard, onions, and crumbled bacon.
3. Heat the beans over the fire, stirring occasionally, for about 15-20 minutes.
4. Serve as a side dish to grilled meats.

Campfire Pizza

Ingredients

- **Pizza dough (store-bought or homemade)**
- **1/2 cup marinara sauce**
- **1 cup shredded mozzarella cheese**
- **Toppings of choice (pepperoni, mushrooms, peppers, etc.)**
- **Olive oil for brushing**

Instructions

1. Roll out the pizza dough to fit your campfire cooking pan or grill.
2. Preheat the grill or campfire.
3. Place the dough on the grill and cook for 2-3 minutes on one side.
4. Flip the dough and spread with marinara sauce, then top with cheese and your favorite toppings.
5. Close the grill or cover with foil and cook for an additional 5-7 minutes until the cheese is melted and bubbly.
6. Serve hot!

Grilled Shrimp Tacos

Ingredients

- 1 lb shrimp, peeled and deveined
- 1 tbsp olive oil
- 1 tsp chili powder
- 1 tsp garlic powder
- 1/2 tsp cumin
- Juice of 1 lime
- Tortillas (for serving)
- Shredded cabbage or lettuce
- Sour cream or salsa for topping

Instructions

1. Preheat the grill or campfire.
2. Toss the shrimp with olive oil, chili powder, garlic powder, cumin, and lime juice.
3. Grill the shrimp for 2-3 minutes per side, until pink and cooked through.
4. Serve in tortillas with shredded cabbage or lettuce, sour cream, and salsa.

Campfire Corn on the Cob

Ingredients

- 4 ears of corn, husked
- 1 tbsp butter per ear
- Salt to taste

Instructions

1. Preheat your grill or campfire.
2. Place the corn directly on the grill or wrap each ear in foil with a tablespoon of butter.
3. Grill for 10-12 minutes, turning occasionally, until the corn is tender and lightly charred.
4. Remove from the fire, add salt, and serve.

Sausage and Potato Hash

Ingredients

- 4 sausages (any variety)
- 2 medium potatoes, diced
- 1 onion, chopped
- 1 bell pepper, chopped
- Salt and pepper to taste
- 1 tbsp olive oil

Instructions

1. Preheat the campfire or grill.
2. In a skillet, cook the sausages until browned and cooked through. Remove and slice into pieces.
3. In the same skillet, sauté the potatoes until golden and cooked through, adding olive oil as needed.
4. Add the onions, bell peppers, sausage pieces, salt, and pepper, and cook for an additional 5-7 minutes.
5. Serve hot as a hearty campfire meal.

Campfire Grilled Cheese

Ingredients

- 4 slices bread
- 2 tbsp butter
- 4 slices cheese (cheddar, American, or your choice)

Instructions

1. Preheat a skillet or grill.
2. Butter one side of each slice of bread.
3. Place the cheese between two slices of bread, with the buttered sides facing out.
4. Grill the sandwich for 2-3 minutes per side until the bread is golden and the cheese is melted.
5. Serve hot with tomato soup or alone for a classic campfire meal.

Dutch Oven Mac and Cheese

Ingredients

- 1 lb elbow macaroni
- 4 cups shredded cheddar cheese
- 2 cups milk
- 2 tbsp butter
- 2 tbsp flour
- Salt and pepper to taste

Instructions

1. Cook the macaroni in a pot over the campfire according to package instructions. Drain.
2. In a Dutch oven, melt the butter and whisk in the flour to make a roux.
3. Slowly add the milk, stirring constantly, until the sauce thickens.
4. Add the shredded cheese, salt, and pepper, stirring until the cheese melts.
5. Mix the cooked macaroni into the cheese sauce and cook for 5-10 minutes, stirring occasionally.
6. Serve hot!

Campfire Apple Crisp

Ingredients

- 4 apples, peeled and sliced
- 1/2 cup rolled oats
- 1/3 cup brown sugar
- 1/4 cup flour
- 1/4 tsp cinnamon
- 1/4 tsp nutmeg
- 1/4 cup butter, diced
- Pinch of salt

Instructions

1. Preheat your campfire or grill to medium heat.
2. In a bowl, combine the apples, brown sugar, cinnamon, nutmeg, and flour.
3. Place the apple mixture in a large piece of foil, spreading it evenly.
4. In a separate bowl, combine the oats, butter, and salt, then sprinkle it over the apples.
5. Fold the foil into a packet and cook over the campfire for 20-25 minutes, checking for doneness.
6. Serve warm, optionally with a scoop of vanilla ice cream.

Campfire Burgers

Ingredients

- 1 lb ground beef
- 1 tsp garlic powder
- 1 tsp onion powder
- Salt and pepper to taste
- 4 burger buns
- Toppings (cheese, lettuce, tomato, ketchup, mustard, etc.)

Instructions

1. Preheat your grill or campfire.
2. In a bowl, season the ground beef with garlic powder, onion powder, salt, and pepper.
3. Shape the beef into 4 patties.
4. Grill the patties for 4-5 minutes per side or until cooked to your desired level of doneness.
5. Toast the burger buns on the grill for 1-2 minutes.
6. Assemble the burgers with your favorite toppings and serve hot.

Grilled Veggie Tacos

Ingredients

- 1 zucchini, sliced
- 1 red bell pepper, sliced
- 1 onion, sliced
- 1 tbsp olive oil
- 1 tsp cumin
- 1 tsp chili powder
- Salt and pepper to taste
- Corn tortillas
- Toppings (sour cream, salsa, cilantro, etc.)

Instructions

1. Preheat your grill or campfire.
2. Toss the vegetables in olive oil, cumin, chili powder, salt, and pepper.
3. Grill the vegetables for 5-7 minutes, turning occasionally, until tender and charred.
4. Warm the tortillas on the grill for 1-2 minutes.
5. Fill the tortillas with the grilled vegetables and top with sour cream, salsa, and cilantro.

Foil Pack Salmon

Ingredients

- 2 salmon fillets
- 1 lemon, sliced
- 2 cloves garlic, minced
- 1 tbsp olive oil
- Fresh herbs (dill, parsley, or thyme)
- Salt and pepper to taste

Instructions

1. Preheat your grill or campfire.
2. Lay each salmon fillet on a large piece of foil.
3. Drizzle with olive oil, and season with minced garlic, salt, and pepper.
4. Top with lemon slices and fresh herbs.
5. Fold the foil into a packet and grill for 15-20 minutes, until the salmon is cooked through.
6. Serve with a side of grilled vegetables or rice.

Quick Camping Stir-Fry

Ingredients

- 2 cups mixed frozen vegetables
- 1 lb chicken breast or beef, sliced thin
- 2 tbsp soy sauce
- 1 tbsp olive oil
- 1 tsp garlic powder
- 1 tsp ginger powder
- Cooked rice (optional)

Instructions

1. Preheat a skillet or wok over the campfire.
2. Heat the olive oil and add the sliced chicken or beef, cooking for 5-7 minutes.
3. Add the mixed vegetables, soy sauce, garlic powder, and ginger powder.
4. Stir-fry for another 5-7 minutes, until the vegetables are tender.
5. Serve over rice, if desired.

Campfire Popcorn

Ingredients

- 1/2 cup popcorn kernels
- 2 tbsp butter
- Salt to taste

Instructions

1. Preheat a pot or campfire popcorn popper over the flames.
2. Add the popcorn kernels and butter.
3. Cover with a lid and shake gently over the fire as the kernels pop.
4. Once the popping slows, remove from the heat and season with salt.
5. Serve hot.

Grilled Sausage and Veggie Skewers

Ingredients

- 4 sausages (any variety), sliced into chunks
- 1 red bell pepper, chopped
- 1 zucchini, sliced
- 1 onion, chopped
- 1 tbsp olive oil
- Salt and pepper to taste

Instructions

1. Preheat the grill or campfire.
2. Thread the sausage and veggies onto skewers, alternating the pieces.
3. Brush with olive oil and season with salt and pepper.
4. Grill the skewers for 8-10 minutes, turning occasionally, until the sausages are cooked through and the veggies are tender.
5. Serve with mustard or your favorite dipping sauce.

Campfire Breakfast Skillet

Ingredients

- 4 eggs
- 1 potato, diced
- 1/2 cup bell pepper, chopped
- 1/4 cup onion, chopped
- 1/4 cup cheese, shredded
- 1 tbsp olive oil
- Salt and pepper to taste

Instructions

1. Preheat a skillet over the campfire.
2. Heat the olive oil and add the diced potato, cooking for 5-7 minutes until soft.
3. Add the bell pepper and onion, cooking for an additional 2-3 minutes.
4. Crack the eggs into the skillet and cook to your desired doneness.
5. Top with cheese and season with salt and pepper.
6. Serve hot for a hearty breakfast.

Baked Sweet Potatoes on the Grill

Ingredients

- 4 sweet potatoes
- 1 tbsp olive oil
- Salt and pepper to taste

Instructions

1. Preheat the grill or campfire to medium heat.
2. Pierce each sweet potato several times with a fork.
3. Rub with olive oil and season with salt and pepper.
4. Wrap the sweet potatoes in foil and place them on the grill.
5. Grill for 40-45 minutes, turning occasionally, until tender when pierced with a fork.
6. Serve with butter or your favorite toppings.

Campfire Casserole

Ingredients

- 1 lb ground beef
- 1 can cream of mushroom soup
- 1 cup frozen mixed vegetables
- 2 cups shredded cheese
- 4 large potatoes, peeled and diced
- Salt and pepper to taste
- 1/2 cup milk

Instructions

1. Preheat your campfire or grill.
2. In a large bowl, mix the ground beef, cream of mushroom soup, mixed vegetables, cheese, and milk.
3. Layer the diced potatoes in the bottom of a foil pan.
4. Pour the beef and vegetable mixture over the potatoes.
5. Cover the pan with foil and cook over the campfire for 25-30 minutes, checking occasionally.
6. Serve warm and enjoy!

Grilled Pineapple with Honey

Ingredients

- 1 fresh pineapple, peeled and sliced into rings
- 2 tbsp honey
- 1 tsp cinnamon

Instructions

1. Preheat your grill or campfire to medium heat.
2. Brush the pineapple slices with honey and sprinkle with cinnamon.
3. Grill the pineapple for 3-4 minutes on each side until caramelized.
4. Serve as a sweet dessert or side dish.

Campfire Sandwiches

Ingredients

- **4 slices of bread**
- **2 slices of cheese**
- **1/4 lb deli meat (ham, turkey, etc.)**
- **Butter or olive oil**

Instructions

1. Butter the outside of the bread slices.
2. Layer cheese and deli meat on the inside of each sandwich.
3. Place the sandwich in a skillet or grill it over the campfire, cooking until golden brown on both sides and the cheese is melted (about 3-4 minutes per side).
4. Serve warm.

Foil Pack Beef Stew

Ingredients

- 1 lb stew beef, cubed
- 2 potatoes, diced
- 2 carrots, sliced
- 1 onion, chopped
- 1 cup beef broth
- 2 cloves garlic, minced
- Salt and pepper to taste

Instructions

1. Preheat the campfire to medium heat.
2. In a large piece of foil, combine the beef, potatoes, carrots, onion, garlic, and beef broth.
3. Fold the foil into a packet and seal tightly.
4. Cook over the fire for 30-40 minutes, checking for tenderness.
5. Serve hot and enjoy a hearty meal.

Skillet Pineapple Chicken

Ingredients

- 4 boneless, skinless chicken breasts
- 1 can pineapple chunks (drained)
- 1 tbsp soy sauce
- 2 tbsp honey
- 1 tbsp olive oil
- Salt and pepper to taste

Instructions

1. Heat the skillet over the campfire and add olive oil.
2. Season the chicken breasts with salt and pepper, then cook in the skillet for 5-7 minutes on each side until golden brown.
3. Add the pineapple, soy sauce, and honey to the skillet.
4. Cook for another 5-7 minutes, allowing the chicken to absorb the flavors.
5. Serve with a side of rice or veggies.

Camping Caesar Salad

Ingredients

- 1 head romaine lettuce, chopped
- 1/2 cup croutons
- 1/4 cup grated Parmesan cheese
- 1/4 cup Caesar dressing

Instructions

1. In a large bowl, combine the chopped lettuce, croutons, and Parmesan cheese.
2. Drizzle with Caesar dressing and toss to coat.
3. Serve immediately as a fresh, easy salad.

Grilled Garlic Bread

Ingredients

- 4 slices of bread
- 2 tbsp butter
- 2 cloves garlic, minced
- 1 tbsp parsley, chopped

Instructions

1. Preheat the grill or campfire.
2. Mix the butter, garlic, and parsley in a small bowl.
3. Spread the garlic butter mixture on one side of each bread slice.
4. Grill the bread for 2-3 minutes on each side until crispy and golden.
5. Serve with your favorite meal.

Campfire Apple Pie

Ingredients

- 2 pre-made pie crusts
- 4 apples, peeled and sliced
- 1/2 cup sugar
- 1 tsp cinnamon
- 2 tbsp butter

Instructions

1. Preheat the campfire to medium heat.
2. In a bowl, combine the apples, sugar, and cinnamon.
3. Roll out the pie crust and line a pie dish with one crust.
4. Fill with the apple mixture and dot with butter.
5. Top with the second crust and seal the edges.
6. Bake in the campfire for 30-40 minutes, checking for golden-brown crust and tender apples.
7. Serve warm with vanilla ice cream.

Easy Grilled Pork Chops

Ingredients

- 4 boneless pork chops
- 1 tbsp olive oil
- 1 tbsp soy sauce
- 1 tsp garlic powder
- 1 tsp onion powder
- Salt and pepper to taste

Instructions

1. Preheat your grill or campfire to medium heat.
2. In a small bowl, mix olive oil, soy sauce, garlic powder, onion powder, salt, and pepper.
3. Brush the pork chops with the marinade mixture.
4. Grill the chops for 6-8 minutes per side until cooked through.
5. Serve with grilled vegetables or a fresh salad.

Campfire Ribs

Ingredients

- 2 racks of baby back ribs
- 1/4 cup BBQ sauce
- 1 tbsp olive oil
- Salt and pepper to taste

Instructions

1. Preheat your grill or campfire to medium-low heat.
2. Rub the ribs with olive oil, salt, and pepper.
3. Place the ribs on the grill, bone side down, and cook for 1-1.5 hours, turning occasionally.
4. Brush with BBQ sauce in the last 10 minutes of cooking.
5. Serve with coleslaw or baked beans.

Dutch Oven Beef Stew

Ingredients

- 1 lb beef stew meat, cubed
- 2 potatoes, diced
- 2 carrots, sliced
- 1 onion, chopped
- 3 cups beef broth
- 2 cloves garlic, minced
- Salt and pepper to taste
- 2 tbsp olive oil

Instructions

1. Preheat your campfire to medium heat.
2. Heat olive oil in the Dutch oven over the campfire and brown the beef stew meat.
3. Add the onions and garlic, cooking until softened.
4. Pour in the beef broth, potatoes, carrots, salt, and pepper.
5. Cover and simmer for 45 minutes to 1 hour, stirring occasionally, until the beef is tender and the vegetables are cooked through.
6. Serve hot and enjoy!

Grilled Peppers and Onions

Ingredients

- 2 bell peppers, sliced
- 1 onion, sliced
- 2 tbsp olive oil
- 1 tsp garlic powder
- Salt and pepper to taste

Instructions

1. Preheat your grill or campfire.
2. Toss the peppers and onions with olive oil, garlic powder, salt, and pepper.
3. Grill the veggies for 5-7 minutes, stirring occasionally, until tender and slightly charred.
4. Serve as a side dish or with tacos, sandwiches, or burgers.

Campfire Frittata

Ingredients

- 6 eggs
- 1/2 cup milk
- 1/2 cup cheese (cheddar or mozzarella), shredded
- 1/2 cup diced ham or bacon (optional)
- 1 cup vegetables (bell peppers, spinach, mushrooms, etc.), chopped
- Salt and pepper to taste

Instructions

1. Preheat your campfire or grill.
2. In a bowl, whisk together the eggs, milk, cheese, salt, and pepper.
3. Heat a cast-iron skillet or Dutch oven over the fire.
4. Sauté the vegetables (and meat if using) in the skillet for 5 minutes.
5. Pour the egg mixture into the skillet and cook over the fire for 10-15 minutes until the eggs are set.
6. Serve and enjoy a hearty breakfast!

Grilled Avocados with Salsa

Ingredients

- 2 avocados, halved and pitted
- 1 tbsp olive oil
- Salt and pepper to taste
- 1/2 cup salsa
- Lime wedges for serving

Instructions

1. Preheat the grill or campfire to medium heat.
2. Brush the cut sides of the avocado with olive oil and season with salt and pepper.
3. Place the avocados, cut side down, on the grill and cook for 3-4 minutes.
4. Top with salsa and serve with lime wedges for a refreshing snack or appetizer.

Campfire Beef Tacos

Ingredients

- 1 lb ground beef
- 1 packet taco seasoning
- 1/2 cup water
- 8 small flour tortillas
- Toppings: lettuce, cheese, salsa, sour cream, etc.

Instructions

1. In a skillet over the campfire, cook the ground beef until browned.
2. Drain any excess fat and stir in the taco seasoning and water.
3. Simmer for 5-10 minutes, until the mixture thickens.
4. Warm the tortillas on the grill or campfire.
5. Assemble tacos with the beef and desired toppings. Serve and enjoy!

Quick and Easy Trail Mix

Ingredients

- 1 cup nuts (almonds, peanuts, cashews, etc.)
- 1/2 cup dried fruit (raisins, cranberries, apricots, etc.)
- 1/4 cup chocolate chips or M&M's
- 1/4 cup sunflower seeds or pumpkin seeds

Instructions

1. In a large bowl, mix together all ingredients.
2. Store in an airtight container or bag for easy snacking while hiking or camping.

Campfire Fried Rice

Ingredients

- 2 cups cooked rice (preferably cold)
- 2 tbsp soy sauce
- 1 tbsp sesame oil
- 1/2 cup frozen peas and carrots
- 2 eggs, scrambled
- 2 green onions, sliced
- Salt and pepper to taste

Instructions

1. Heat the sesame oil in a skillet over the campfire.
2. Add the peas and carrots and cook for 3-4 minutes.
3. Push the vegetables to one side and scramble the eggs on the other side of the skillet.
4. Add the cooked rice and soy sauce, mixing everything together.
5. Cook for 5-7 minutes, stirring occasionally.
6. Top with green onions and serve warm.

Grilled Bananas with Chocolate

Ingredients

- 2 ripe bananas
- 1/4 cup chocolate chips
- 1/4 cup marshmallows

Instructions

1. Preheat the grill or campfire.
2. Slice the bananas in half lengthwise, leaving the peel on.
3. Place chocolate chips and marshmallows in the center of each banana half.
4. Wrap the bananas in foil and grill for 5-7 minutes until the chocolate and marshmallows are melted.
5. Serve immediately for a sweet treat!

Foil Pack Veggie Stir-Fry

Ingredients

- 1 cup mixed vegetables (broccoli, bell peppers, zucchini, etc.)
- 1 tbsp olive oil
- 2 tbsp soy sauce
- 1 tsp garlic powder
- Salt and pepper to taste

Instructions

1. Preheat the campfire to medium heat.
2. Toss the mixed vegetables with olive oil, soy sauce, garlic powder, salt, and pepper.
3. Wrap the veggies in foil and cook over the fire for 10-15 minutes until tender.
4. Serve as a side dish or with rice.

S'mores Nachos

Ingredients

- **Tortilla chips**
- **1 cup mini marshmallows**
- **1/2 cup chocolate chips**
- **1/4 cup peanut butter (optional)**

Instructions

1. Preheat the campfire or grill.
2. Spread tortilla chips in a foil pan or cast-iron skillet.
3. Top with marshmallows and chocolate chips (and peanut butter if using).
4. Place the pan over the campfire and cook for 5-7 minutes until the chocolate is melted and the marshmallows are golden brown.
5. Serve with a spoon and enjoy a fun twist on s'mores!

Campfire Spaghetti

Ingredients

- 1 lb spaghetti
- 2 cups marinara sauce
- 1/2 cup grated Parmesan cheese
- Salt and pepper to taste

Instructions

1. Boil water over the campfire in a large pot and cook the spaghetti according to package instructions.
2. While the pasta is cooking, heat the marinara sauce in a separate pot or skillet.
3. Drain the pasta and toss with the sauce.
4. Top with Parmesan cheese and serve hot.

www.ingramcontent.com/pod-product-compliance
Lightning Source LLC
LaVergne TN
LVHW081332060526
838201LV00055B/2603